THE WANDERER

Douglas J. Penick

Mountain Treasury Press

LCCN:2014901834

Mountain Treasury Press, Boulder, CO, USA

ISBN-10: 0974597481

ISBN-13: 978-0974597485

TO SUCH CHANCE ENCOUNTERS
AND SUCH TRUE LOVE

CONTENTS

	Introduction	xi
1	River	1
2	Continuing with: Arakawa	7
3	Elements	25
4	Dream Tiger	33
5	Time's Unending	37
6	Elysium	63
7	You Died, and	69
8	Twilight and History	75
9	Soldier Cry	107
10	The Coming of the Ice Age: Dreams and Sings The Minotaur	121
11	Conscientiousness	135
	Notes	145

INTRODUCTION

Wishes and longings to the contrary, the wanderer does not find lasting rest. Movement is continuous.

Worlds, words, experiences coalesce. A moment engulfs.

In such landings, in such intensities, all is now intimately real. Duration of such inadvertent residing is not in the wanderer's control.

The wanderer waits, is attentive, and surrenders in chance encounters, tales and songs.

DJP 1/15/14

1.

RIVER

for Deborah continuously

1)

Alive

Where solid ground and rushing waters

Have not parted ways:

The river sparkles with the songs and stories of all who live by it: Flowing, flowing with their loves, their battles, their leisure, their work, their gods, their desires flowing with their losses, their endurance, flowing in their loneliness. The river is a song of transformations, ends, creations and time.

Now in verse, the miraculous, Kalidasa evokes the audience listening to a reading of the Ramayana:

"And the people sat beside the river

And they listened,

Enraptured, they listened.

Tears ran down their faces like pearls,

Like dew dripping from the forest leaves

In the stillness of a windless dawn."

2)

And, as if remembering someone they saw on shore

As the river of words carried them on,

They remembered how a king left his palace

How he left his splendid halls.

How he walked deep into the forest shadows

And walked through reeds and swamps.

He came to the great river,

Radiant, enticing, imperious, vast.

And he looked silently

Upon the Ganges flowing through the three times:

Clear, with cool waves loved by sages,

Giving life and dharma to teachers and the places
where they teach.

Song rose in his heart from a distant mountain spring.

He joined his hands in prayer. He sang, and his song

was like a life giving river. He sang, and the sky shone

with his melodious voice.

"O you who are love,

In your clear waters, apsaras play.

"O Ganges of the gods, asuras and gandarvas

Meandering through the endless sky,

"O river of celestial lotuses,

Sacred river, roaring, quivering, smiling

With sparkling teeth of white foam,

Flowing unimpeded,

Curling like a young girl's wind-blown hair;

"O river of swirling whirlpools and peaceful ponds,

Crying river, roiled and unsettling;

Holy river where goddesses bathe

Amid white lotus clouds

And the plangent calls of swans and cranes;

"You are garlanded with dark trees,

Brocaded with green lily pads,

Aflame with red water lilies,

Jeweled with gold and silver dancing light,

Powdered with pink pollen dust,

"Blushing like a longing lover,

Suddenly you draw near, you touch, you whirl away."

3)

Song rose in his heart as from a distant mountain spring. He joined his hands in prayer. He sang, and his song was like a life-giving river. He sang, and the sky shone with his melodious voice.

"You strike the dry land

And ten thousand pearls spray in the air

Rising, rising up in iridescent clouds.

"In every spinning droplet,

The moments of our history,

The moments of time, our life and death,

Shine in the sky, O pearl pure Ganges.

"O pearl pure Ganges,

O river of milk,

O life of all,

O river of blood,

O love,

O ever-flowing one,

"Echoing the future,

Reverberant in full expanse,

You carry off all sin,

All sorrow, all regret."

2.
CONTINUING WITH: ARAKAWA

for Genevieve Kapular and Gianni Longo

The pop of poles pulling from the river bed;

The stagnant smell of river mud;

The fishermen push out through crackling reeds

Into the secret stream.

We lean against the pole,

Entering the drift as a subtle current takes us

And our heart/mind, unsure, relieved,

Surrenders.

*

Well, here we are.

Here. Though this is surely familiar, it may not

be your preferred aesthetic any more. Perhaps,

while it represents for me a freedom, for you

7

perhaps it's imprisonment, cliché. Either way, a

now distant birthplace for us both, I think.

I hope you don't mind.

Certainly, it's not what either of us expected, is it?

I miss you, you know. I miss the possibility of

phone calls which you would have your wife

make when you'd had a dream or an intuition.

Those no more. But here we are and it's better

than nothing, no?

And still, as ever, a surprise.

*

A quick shock

From within, as if a terrible thought,

A premonition,

A cramp

Freezes each in place.

And frozen in that sharp empty moment,

Impenetrable space expands

Pale and black

And so unsure.

Frozen,

Standing in the boat,

No forward motion

But rocking side to side,

Listening as the water laps.

Perhaps a fish has leapt far off.

Looking as if a crane has risen suddenly,

And there is a cause

For this sudden gap.

*

We often share that.

Before we met, the woman who introduced us told me
about you visiting her studio and looking at her paintings.
She heard you saying under your breath: "All that
work....and... For What?"

A tremor of 'for what?' I wanted to meet you then. Now we have just a different kind of meeting, a new relationship to embodiment, I guess we could say. A little strained. Different possibilities. But unsure as ever.

I see you smile. It's not as if you AREN'T exactly,

is it?

*

Do you remember that time you and Agnetti, both nicely drunk, were standing by the kitchen table? Sunset light glowed in the dust streaks on the windows. "You and I... are exactly...the same," you told him carefully, "BUT" and here your eyes rounded in amazement, "...one of us is just a little taller."

So, you're gone, but here we are as again, you, in your chosen conversational format, recount your conversations with others.

As you told me then you'd gone out late one sultry summer night for a walk and ended up chatting with the old Italian men sitting under the limp maple trees on Houston St. just below 6th Avenue.

"When you think about when you were young, is it long ago or like yesterday?" you asked them. "Oh, just like yesterday," they replied gravely.

Your grandmother, do you remember?, gave you a fruit they call now an Asian Pear. When you first saw it, it was just after WWII had ended. Your grandmother showed it to you. It was, she said, very expensive. "What is it?" you asked. "It's a Twentieth Century fruit." "Really?" "Yes." "And do you know why it's called that?" "Why?" "Because this is the Twentieth Century." And she held it out to you. "It's your century."

*

And onward following the meandering stream

That leaves the shadow landscape of familiar scents,

The vague silhouettes of houses

Where neighbors dream,

Barns where ill-fated livestock sleeping

Paw at the earth.

Following on hidden channels, we press on

Sensing growing unfamiliarity,

A strangeness, risk.

The river widens,

Solid land recedes,

And ahead, we intuit wider space,

Mysterious and unconstrained.

*

An early visit took place in summer. In the long cool gray
studio with a cold gray marble floor salvaged from, you
said, a bank, we drank bright red hibiscus tea.

"The difference between Kafka and Mallarme is that Kafka could always pour himself completely into anything he could imagine- a cockroach, anything. In whatever Mallarme imagined, he found only a vast void until even looking in the mirror, all he saw was void and chance."

And soon thereafter, a party filling the same room: Duchamp's sprightly widow, John Cage suffering from arthritis discussing shoes, Jasper Johns aloof, pickled, Raushenberg, garrulous and fun, drinking, telling when first he saw the world with corrective eyeglasses, stripped of the luminous haze and how he was 'ashamed to be in such a place'.

And late one night, you told me how you saw the art world consumed with cynicism, greed and stripped of morals, offering nothing to those who followed. We talked about Liberace and his sincerity.

*

Then your art: your maps. These diagrams

marking the field or pathway from:

"Whenever "I" or "we" is pronounced, it feels

or seems as though there will follow full presence

of a subject in addition to that of the speaker.

We are given only shifting space or a field of play....

"I have begun to consider the construction

of a situation for a parallel, reminiscent

of Frankenstein, as a strong way to respond

to the nonsensical urgency of subject matter. ...

"Always we are used-up texture, then we

become texture... (but) to make the maximum situation:

"1. Two or thee points of departure

"2. Edge blank

(describe)

"3. Receivability

"4. By: enclosure for continuance(?).

"5. Saturation vectors" and these on through

"6. Layered approximations…"

And continuing to

"19. Diffuse receding

"20. Waiting texture

"21. Impressionable stretching…"

until finally you reached

"32. Sudden drop…

"33. Scale of action… "

and ended with – on that occasion-

"34. Call of continuity: the momentum or the maker of
second nature: energy advisor: judge?" *

And these spread and placed within a vast expanse
of wonder: schematic drawings as balanced as
askew, suggesting a continuing into time and on.
This world you articulate is for me always
quizzical, fresh and a happy return into the secret stream.

*

Blurred and shimmering inside warm billowing clouds.

A sound expanding in the still night,

And a sky is filled with starless light.

Entering the drift as a subtle current takes us

And our heart/mind, unsure, relieved,

Surrenders.

*

Of course, years of practice made the detailed terrain of such tracking almost familiar. Longchen Rabjam would have been quite happy sitting with you here.

Remember when I asked you if you had ever considered living, practicing in a formal Buddhist framework?

"Oh yes," you said. You had gone to a Zen monastery for a six-week probationary training. At the end, the abbot expelled you, saying you had "Too many thoughts." Do you remember the terrible sob that wrenched from your heart when you told me this? I can hear it even now.

And so you have discovered, if not a new stream, a new mapping.

You are close to me right now, as an elder

brother, moving through the dark always just

within view. Right now.

*

Do you remember our conversation about the

great antipathy all the surrealists had to taking

taxis? Eluard's widow was scandalized that you

would even consider it even though the Metro

had closed for the night. This emerging from

one of many long chats about Nicolas Calas

who had just been mugged in the subway.

*

My father died suddenly and, in the same week, your father

died. You and your father had been estranged. He was a

doctor and had been a Soviet prisoner of war after they

took Manuchuria. He had been locked in the bottom of a

latrine for months. He had never been the same. Still you

spoke of him and held my hand, thinking of my father too; their deaths: "a terrible inconceivable tragedy." You shook your head.

I asked you about your mother. You described her as old, a little crazy. She showed you how every morning she went outside and, arms upraised greeted the sun as it rose. "You don't have to do that," you told her. "You're still young," she snapped back. "What do you know?"

*

In the darkness moving quietly through lapping water
Unseen

What knowing is there?

Moving forward, what traces to what goal?

What can be told that can be followed or count as useful knowing?

And yet…
Could we stop in such endeavor?

Could we stop and still count ourselves among
the living?

*

Do you remember? The French Government
wanted to make you a Chevalier du Legion de
L'Art. "What is that," you asked. "Something
to do with horses, yes?" They explained it
was an honor. "But what's it good for?" You
asked nicely. "Well, it helps with reservations
in restaurants and hotels." "Ok."

And then, at the ceremony where you received this honor,
you gave a speech in which you said that in the 20th
Century, every concept, every emotional arrangement,
every belief, every theory of social, psychological, ethical or
physical reality had created nothing but one huge total
disaster. You proposed that the only solution now was to
consider low-income housing.

Soon after that you decided to abandon making your wonderful maps, and make buildings in which where the maps led to could be realized directly by the occupants.

It was at that time you began to believe that the rearrangement of percept and perceiver was sufficient to overcome death. As if this were volitional act.

Completely rearranging what the compositors of the Abidharma called co-dependent origination would allow for such a shift in mortality, but composite phenomena being by their nature inherently unstable, not for its termination.

Your wife responded to this objection with

anger. You merely laughed and said: "You agree

that living in such a building could prolong life,

yes? ... Well, why not go a little further."

*

Now we pole our vessels onward.

It is not yet time to write the poems of parting.

I hear you whistle through your teeth.

I hear the water hiss

Deeper than notions of destiny.

I hear you laugh.

What termination of affection, of understanding, of quest

Has been effected here?

What does it mean, this death you opposed?

*

Do you remember the last time I saw you. The last time I

saw you, your wife handed me a card that said: "Make

Death Illegal". "Oooh" I said, "Are you contemplating a

medical or legal initiative here? I think the former will

work better, since there really is no effective punishment you can impose in the latter." You laughed and invited me for tea; your wife looked unhappy.

I was so glad to see you. Do you remember that I asked where love fit in your endeavor? You looked down and did not answer. I'm still asking you, beloved brother.

*

We shall speak of this again.

3.

ELEMENTS

for Kenneth H. Green

To wake from a dream

Where hundreds of friends

Read aloud in concert

A new and unknown poem

Of which remains:

"The condition of work is always for us

To endure the threat to the body's frame."

II)

Point suddenly appearing

4 A.M.

Above the street that shines in rain,

Rusts in the tawny glare of the sodium lights –
Lifeless;

And the rain blown in sharp gusts
By the fine aromatic breeze of rising spring,
Blown then in waves articulate on the glass

Such that

The water strikes on the pane silently,
Adheres dot-wise, slides forming shoots
Of golden light diagonal.

And within each shoot gilded by the tawdry light
Each atom-drop breathes like a cell –
Not substance,
Of no duration,
Continual unrest.

And it is so … … … … Dazzling

That further, on the rank street, shinier

With clear white light from their yellow bodies,

Taxis in a row

Disgorge and fetch the haunted wraithlike

     Windblown

Who pursue … … … … … something.

Give my love to you.

III)

Point moving

Thus rise the senses to the invitation

Who themselves are subtle,

Subtle,

Indivisible,

Fireproof,

Weightless, shining like a jewel,

Leaving no residue at death.

IV)

Point seeming to expand

Here the lover

In his cotton bathrobe,

Smoking the illicit cigarette,

Dry-eyed, pale,

A small face to make out in this window

Above the street, above the streetlights even.

Those in hot pursuit below would not see,

But the cigarette smoke rises so pleasantly past

The face and out into the rainy night.

And the ember pulses:

Burn and rest.

How could this not be the dreamy face

Of love itself

Of endless caress.

The elements are energized.

Sudden sheets of fleeting light impelled

As sashes whipped on rushing rain.

The sodium orange light,

Looked at here straight on,

Burns like a Martian sun,

A finger hole of brilliant light

Seen through a tear in a black shade:

Bright beyond the previous reality.

V)

Point seeming to remain

A delight of a sad kind,

Composed of so many blisses:

Intoxicant unfolding

Of the endless, sinuous and purposeless song:

Unlimited variety, balance, adjustment –

Response

As bit by bit

The atoms of all embrace. And vanish

Carrying the lover off.

VI)

Point dissipating

An excess that will not stop

As now he lies in the semi-dark.

The iron basso grinding wheeze

Of foraging garbage trucks

And the treble clinking crunch and tenor crash

As hundreds of glass bottles are consumed

And beast thus fed so roaring on.

This and darkness now becoming pale

Silence briefly,

Before the varied hiss of orderly flow,

When the lover sleeps

And the workers return.

4.
DREAM TIGER

for John Perks

The reader, sleeping, wandered through a dense, light-dappled rainforest. At a bend in the path, he found himself suddenly on the banks of a sluggish stream. Across the stream in deeper shadows, he could see a twig hut with palm-leaf roof. An old woman, cross-eyed, with dark, dusty skin and dirty, matted hair, sat on the ground in front of the hut. Her half-demented smile, as she glanced up at him, revealed a mouthful of broken teeth. With a skeletal right hand, she lifted a copper water pot to her mouth and drank. The water dribbled from the corners of her mouth, down her neck and along her dried up breasts.

She hummed contentedly to herself. Suddenly she looked directly at the reader. She stared and leered as she ran her black tongue slowly across her cracked lips.

The reader was embarrassed. He felt like a peeping-tom and was filled with indecision, even panic. He did not want to be involved in any way with this crazy person, but he was caught by a certain disgusted fascination. His only alternative was to run away, but that would be even more embarrassing.

As he stood there fixed, all at once he noticed an enormous tiger prowling fluidly through the shadows, moving slowly towards the woman from behind her hut. The reader had seen tigers before: locked in cages, chained at palace gates, and even far off in the wild. But nothing prepared him for the immense sinuous power of the beast or the splendid opulence of its black stripes and orange fur. He felt himself reflected in the rapacious intelligence of its golden eyes. He thought he could feel the heat of its blood-scented breath, pulsing past the gleaming fangs and hard black lips, burning on his face.

Unconcerned as the tiger crept close behind her, the old woman continued to stare at him, running her left hand up and down the inside of her thigh in a revolting and unmistakable gesture of sexual invitation.

Before the reader could react or shout a warning, the tiger shot out from the underbrush and leapt into the air. In one bound, the beast flew over the old woman, over the flat earth where she sat, over the river, and dropped, hot mouth gaping over the spell-bound reader. He passed out and felt as if he was swallowed into the black steaming void of the creature's maw. He was tumbling in the dark, beyond fear, pain, death. The tiger had devoured him, the old woman, the hut, the jungle, everything.

He felt a stream of cool water trickle down his throat, and he woke. His head lay in the hag's lap. Seen up close, her dark skin glowed like polished leather. She smelled pleasantly of cinnamon. She smiled tenderly at him as she carefully poured water from the copper pot onto his lips. The tiger, calm and majestic, sat curled around the hag at her back. From time to time, he idly licked her shoulder, leaving a slight trail of spit. Though everything was simple and clear, the reader was confused.

"There isn't any mystery here," said the hag in a soft, light youthful voice. "You experienced this."

Then, he was seated before her, and she stretched out her palm as if offering him something. At the same time, it seemed she might be about to ask a question.

But just before the reader could think of what he might say or ask or answer, she swung the copper pot in a swift arc and struck him hard on the head. There was an engulfing metallic thunk, a sudden burst of pain, and the reader lost consciousness.

5.
TIME'S UNENDING

Again for Deborah and ever onward

1)

A life is spent in unconscious subservience

To the demands of living,

To the demands of striving: conquest, release,
acceptance, final love.

A life is spent in unconscious subservience

To the demands imposed by the beautiful flowering

Of our passage through existing.

Life bears down on us

As we move into the landscape of loss.

Pulled down by the gravity

Of times that will not return and not continue,

We slowly crumble and move slowly

Into a white desert without horizon.

It begins and continues.

It continues

Opening an expanse of white light:

Time without chronology.

Birds we cannot see are singing in an unending dawn.

We do not understand.

Passage without beginning or end.

Sheer continuing.

First and finally he recognizes it.

2)

The life of an old man is ending.

Exiled from Greece, exiled from Paris, exiled from those, now dead who so admired his complex poems, his brilliant essays, he is trapped outside the world that once found him so splendid, a world that now is almost gone.

"How are you?" I ask. Though it is late afternoon, he is seated on his unmade bed, unshaven, not yet fully dressed.

"Nonexistent."

"And how is that?"

"I have reached another stage."

"Ah."

"I've lost interest."

"I see."

We sit together and drink tea out of not very clean cups. His wife stirs angrily in the bedroom, cursing in Russian. He makes no effort at conversation. Then

"I am dying." We look at each other for a while until he turns away.

"Are you apprehensive?" I ask.

"Somewhat." Another long pause. "You see, I've made a mistake."

"What's that?"

"What I told you before."

"The losing interest?"

"Yes."

Often as I sit with him in his final decline, I sense that we are sitting on a bleak shore by an oily gray exhausted sea as fleeting images, bits of memory, half-remembered phrases bob in the feeble waves. I try to interest him in using these fragments to write poems once again. He won't.

I write the poem myself. He does not respond. He looks out the window at a yellowing tree as I read this to him.

3)

Non-Existence

No.

No peace with that.

The habit of thought

Arises in response

To an unmade bed;

Tea with a small amount of milk,

Husky Russian vowels amid the kitchen crockery.

The lure of tonalities rise

Like the memory of a white sky above a purple sea:

A breeze from the shore of the exile's homeland

Where culture vanished long ago but remained

Enough to mirror, in a delicate and incisive way,

The great doings

Of brasher nations on the go.

Still a vague yearning for the atmosphere

Of a pale horizon poised on promise.

But seated in shadow on remembered subway steps

A charcoal-black man

Suggests the sultry wealth of Africa

And dark barbarian threat.

Again the familiar tickle of a riddle

Beloved

Teasing to continue –

What?

To continue

In the familiar and seductive texture

Of what can be said and still resists being known:

The tip of a tongue.

Still yours?

Desiring, at the wet tip of a tongue

To taste continuing desire,

So subtly to be loved.

In form that increasingly eludes

Form

Like the pink opalescence

Shifting in a bank of clouds above the sea.

The skin of experience adheres

To the habits of mind

Knowing and being known:

Waves thus watch waves

Dancing light in light.

The question

Questioning

Questioner

Dissolves enigmatically

As a sparkling play

In a luminous sea that never was,

That was never known by anyone,

That never began,

Nor never ceased:

Resting an exhausted mind

In that.

Love to you.

4)

Now the trap is closing.

Circumstances can't be changed.

A twinge, a shadow

Waits to transform everything from inside out.

Soon enough, the pain that will not stop,

The illness that can't be cured.

Will take control of him from inside out.

A shadow will engulf the world

And cast its own light.

Everything now glows in the raking light of a failing
sun.

A towering gold cloud,

A meadowlark deep in shadowed purple woods,

His wife's quick smile,

Leaves turning into orange flames,

A crow in flight,

Cars whispering homeward,

The smell of wood smoke,

Her smooth back.

The thought of travel.

All shine on the edge of disappearing.

Impossibly alive.

Intensities now framed by impending loss.

Mind cannot stop.

Transformations now cannot be foreseen.

We sit unmoving. We make no effort but we are watching. Like waiting for a snow lion to emerge from the pine forest, we sit still and we watch. Poised, we wait.

A subtle stream is flowing all around us. Thoughts rise in our minds. Hopes and fears are coloring our feeling. Slight aches flicker in our body. We do not move, and, one by one, each transient movement of our mind is carried off. Every apprehension, every bright plan, every hidden yearning moves on the flow of an invisible stream. Appearing and disappearing. Every occurrence, every feeling, cherished or despised, appears and is carried away. We are sitting in the vast river of time.

Time itself is flowing through us. Moments move and coalesce. They make, in passing by, the shape we call ourselves. They flow past and separate. Each moment moves away, is carried off, dissolves.

Something is lost; something unexpected is taking shape.

On the flow of disappearing, a mist, a shadow hovers. Gone beyond remembering, new beyond knowing, it plays on the liquid surface. It whispers new secrets within each moment of total loss.

5)

Somewhere inside our skin, it is waiting for us.

A stranger will appear within our body like a shadow beside a staircase. Suddenly a chill, a cellular awakening: a kind of knowing.   We turn away. We look at something else. But we know.

Without words,

The faint snow mountains and fragrant pines

Call.

Without light,

The black night sky

Dreams.

Thus we know

And speak with the living and the dead,

Held in their hidden love.

The faint scent of skin

Fades in the dark amid golden leaves

Outside about to fall.

A moon not full,

Yet bright as if full,

Floods the sky

And reveals a long luminous cloud bank,

Like a new snow-mountain range

Rising on horizon's edge.

Another world

Now opens here.

6)

The life of a middle-aged_man is ending. He looks out at the highway from his hospital bed.

"I'm a little behind the curve," he shrugs.

"Yes?"

"There is something so .. big... in this dissolving. Not so frightening, but so... big, and so..." He hovers there, circling his pale hand slowly, and looks at me to see if I understand. It all feels surprisingly normal.

He nods. And together in the dim hospital room, we are floating in a space so neutral and blank, but where, at the same time, it seems everything could in an instant dissolve or, in the very same instant, change or be born completely anew. I don't know how long we drift in this way, but it is companionable, easy, slightly humorous. Then interrupted by the rolling rattling and clatter of the food cart.

A skinny Afro-American in green scrubs and a white hair-net looks at him and then at a metal clipboard.

"Solid food. No restrictions?" He says this as if it was somehow all that mattered. My dying friend gives a slow gracious nod. The aide slaps the white plastic tray with its plastic wrapped utensils and glass, bottled water, cellophane encased roll, and meal and dessert each under a metal lid which the aide lifts and takes away. My friend is spellbound and does not reply.

His attention to the items on the tray before him is rapt. From time to time, his eyebrows raise as some particularly strange item catches his eye. Sometimes, slowly he purses his lips. It's like watching an alien arrive from outer space and try to figure out what these objects, so routine in terrestrial existence, do and mean. He is patient and circumspect. He does not touch the items before him until he has examined them carefully. He shakes his head and looks up at me with a shrug and a smile as if we were sharing a joke.

Wherever my friend is at this moment is highly communicative. We share the centerless strangeness of it all: the hospital smell, bed, food, noise and whispers in Spanish from the corridor, all unaccountable and profoundly disorienting. Everything is suspended in a state of gentle bemusement as he explores the circumstance of cautiously tasting gravy, potatoes, corn, milk. This state expands when a young doctor enters with a nurse and a young woman in business-like suit and ring binder, the social worker.

They begin to explain that tomorrow my friend, his family and the doctors will meet to determine if treatment should continue. The young doctor asks if there is anything he would like to discuss now. My friend nods gravely, and after a minute or so begins speaking. He talks slowly with long pauses.

"It is, you know, ... not much better to discover within one's ... carcass new resources for ...application than to discover ... the absence of them. ... Their being new doesn't ...somehow... add ... at all ... to their interest but makes them... stale and flat, ... as if one had long ago exhausted them. ..."

He stops and takes a long breath. The doctor is mesmerized and the nurse and social worker who had both begun by taking notes find themselves immobilized.

We are all carried on his words, words that verge on meaning nothing but continue to unfold as if they rise from somewhere. on the far edge of the horizon before slowly disappearing and keep us suspended as they pass. The sounds of the other patients, the hospital have faded. He looks at each of us earnestly.

"Such is my sketchy state of... mind, ... but I feel sure I shall discover plenty of fresh... oh ... worlds to conquer, even if I am to be cheated... yes, that's the word... of the amusement of them."

He goes on in this way for almost ten minutes holding us powerless the whole time. It is strange and wonderful. But suddenly the doctor shakes his head and looks at his watch. The two women stare at each other as if waking from a dream. My friend smiles brightly as abruptly they leave.

7)

We sit and watch.

Time flows through us. The conjunction of moments, physical, emotional, historical, that we have come to call ourselves is dissolving and reforming.

The one who is watching is not one whom we know. The one who is watching is also slipping off, like a shimmering bubble, rushing by, dodging the solid rocks, changing shape with flow and plunging into tumbling rapids. The watcher is evolving and changing to something unfamiliar, someone new.

Suddenly overcome by fear and regret and the urgent need to slow such headlong continuing, we get up. Something needs to be done. The lights need to be turned on. A glass of water. Something is needed. We seek escape in solidity. We get up. For a moment, it is not quite so noticeable that time is moving, moving, moving and taking us away, taking us somewhere, somewhere we cannot know.

Mind cannot stop.

Overcome by time and chance, body and faculties are being transformed in ways utterly unforeseen.

Is there a change of allegiance from the desire for permanence to the shifting away?

Our bodies are collapsing slowly in that shift. Our heart/minds are losing their transient forms and boundaries. We are falling in the centerless awareness mind-sky.

8)

Mind is the stream of time. It cannot stop.

Senses, memories, feelings are liberated from specifics. Incomplete histories are liberated and reformed. Re-shaping time is expanding and contracting. Time is freeing itself from itself.

Occurrences past ebb like the ripples in a pond. Slight waves diminishing as they move steadily away. Thoughts disappear like the imprint of birds in the sky. Slowly, slowly, slowly the sky expands pale and silvery-blue.

Names, hallways, chairs, routines, faces fade. Food is good. Gone. The sky is pink and gold. Words do not hold the world together.

The trees are not trees. Green, lush and undulant moments expanding in the river of time that gets slower and slower, wider, deeper and all-encompassing. Something is opening to accept us. A shining ocean from which we have never been separated. A vast sea in which we are coalescing as alone, yet not alone. Our conversation with the world continuing.

As if coming towards us from another world, we see, appearing simultaneously half here and half there, future selves, a self that is and is not one we know. The shadow approaches. A new love strangely altered. We feel the exhilaration of vast possibility. We cannot see the shadow's face. For a moment, we are swallowed by a blue expanse of freezing fear.

6.
ELYSIUM

FOR JOHN SEL

"The fear of you and the dread of you shall be upon every beast of the earth and upon every fowl of the air; upon all that moveth upon the earth and upon all the fishes of the sea. Into your hands they are delivered. Every moving thing that liveth shall be meat for you. " (Genesis IX 2-3)

I

Remembering desiring imagining feeling: how deeply is one seen as self-deceived?

II

Of mute creatures confined in hide and flesh to moo and bellow, low and moan; one outstanding for scruffiness, another for proud command, for warmth and tenderness, for kindness, for a strange scent, for japery or unsociable waywardness, for sudden rage:

What record is there of their herded passing, what tale

63

of traversal on the soil? What voice can tell of the various ways in which one loved and was loved, one knew and was known?

III

Loved perhaps for many reasons, but lives brought forth, nurtured and sustained for the rich red meat to be stripped from their great frames and for the hides that cover them: these to be scoured and tanned to remove the tufty fur which so resembles the stubble ground of harvest fields where these same cattle once grazed.

IV

Patient and enduring, nuzzling slowly, sociable with their dense drizzling noses, herded hither and thither as the convenience of the little killer-men dictate, so to wander in groups gathering and dispersing, each impressive volume on broad hooved feet, miring up the hock, sinking firmly in the mud then ambling slowly to higher ground, a particular tuft of straw perceived dimly through white-lashed eye; Up to where the red-gold sun warms through the thick hide, wandering ponderously up to there with grunt and moo and sidewise nudge of herd-mate, strange old friend. And on the crest of the rise, a cooling breeze, cool of evening brings acrid scent of plop and sweet of still warm grass and buzz of blowing fly. Forbearing in these modest happinesses which great bulk and time afford. And pleasantly ignorant of prod and truck and chute and electrode and of knife which shall end in a moment of overwhelming knowingness an idyll on the land.

V

A long social history of them who stretch existence in this slow way of idle days, unknowing servitude but obedient to the longer strand of time which is measured by winter hay on hard ground and by tender grasses returning, measured by time in the winds and rain on broad fields and in the crowded dark of barns, lowering in the comfortable warmth of fellowness. There high in the dark eaves live the flickering swallows dim above them, darting down and near them, a trivial enigma, uninteresting omen.

VI

Though no longer to kick up heels, no longer to flip and flap and roll in clover, nor nudge up close to the great beloved warmth and delve beneath it, there in the best of dark to suck and taste the smooth sweet white flow of sustenance, of milk and love. Gravid now, ponderous and slow-moving, ruminant, measuring in time and slow herd drift the distances between the broad rolling earth and the flocks of pinkish clouds drifting likewise in the sky. Vast satisfaction there in the heavy factuality of that.

VII

But looking to the eye screwing sky-ward in the socket, head slinging back and up, when fear like a cork-screw shall twist out placid sense. What, in warmth was so pleasantly enjoyed: green sour chewing cud or squish in hoof-wide ponds while wandering through rain which dripped off matted flanks, what can prepare for the onslaught of horror impossible to resist, that splits the skull in two like an axe-edge crashing down between the eyes.

VIII

If there is a wind that can take from the body its spirit, does it carry the metal-sharp imminent scent flashing down at them and bring terrible shock to their patient gentle days that have never known its like? Then suddenly aware of all this rolling time as a cruel deception that masked the sordid brutal nature lying on the far side of the enclosed fences where their wanderings stopped. Does this sudden knowing kill as surely as the night to follow?

IX

Sense merged so deeply in this monumental meat and bone, slow to move in this frame adapted to all life of lengthy increase and perambulating interest, disgruntlement and occasional bumbling panic; all life as if there were a measure according to that pace, assumed at the end a certain visionary quality even as it is stripped away.

As if all those afternoons in sun and those morning plodding through mist leaving hoof-prints in the dew, those warm, earth-bound smells of fellowship in the cold of darkest night, all stop. They hover as if there had been a meaning which does not apply to present circumstances. All are now the view of Paradise seen from Hell, blinding in their unity.

7
YOU DIED, AND

In Memory of Peter Lieberson

You died, and three days later:

I found myself in a gray-green sky, high above an ocean the color of green slate. I was piloting a WWII Japanese Zero, and the plane, oddly, was painted the same color as the sea. Far below, I could see one or two bright blue splotches: some kind of boats with white lines of foam trailing behind. I was alone in the misty sky.

I was not aware that I had ever piloted a plane before, but the situation seemed familiar enough. I had a clear memory of appropriating the plane; walking quickly across the tarmac, climbing up on the wing, settling in the cockpit, pulling the canopy forward, taking off; I'd known what to do. I looked over at the fuel gauge:

the hand was fluttering on empty. Yes, that too had been part of the plan.

Now I saw it: apparently it had been my intention all along to crash the plane into the sea, to die. Strange. I felt no anguish, no despair. There was no terrible memory, no ache of inassimilable loss. There was nothing of that kind. I was calm and, as far as I could tell, lucid. I had no strong memories of anything and no strong feelings about what I should be doing. I was just a middle-aged Japanese man, alone in the air. The air around me had the same muted hues as the sea below.

The engine stuttered slightly; fuel was beginning to run out. What was about to happen was suddenly extremely vivid. I saw the plane crash into the sea, felt the sudden pain of being ripped against the seat harness, knew the confusion as water splashed up engulfing the canopy. Even though I had not lost consciousness, I would be too stunned to move. The plane would float for a moment before tipping forward and begin its slow sinking. Slowly the light would darken above me. The air trapped inside the canopy would allow me to continue breathing. Soon water would begin to leak in a little at first, then more.

The engine coughed and shuddered, the nose dropped forward, and the plane began to fall from the sky. I was suddenly aware of my own claustrophobia. I knew that I would be unable to prevent myself from struggling against the leather harness, fumbling uncontrollably with the buckles. I could see myself clawing to release the canopy, even as the massed weight of the sea held it in place. I could hear my gasping, and see my mind go wild. It was very clear.

I pulled on the controls to lift the plane's nose, to allow it to glide for as long as possible. I did not think I'd had a change of heart or discovered some desire to live; I simply did not wish, if I could help it, to die in the way I'd just foreseen.

When the plane began to descend, I steered it into a broad lateral arc. There was, strictly speaking, no advantage in doing this. I simply liked the idea of moving through the air in this way. Wisps of fog blew past. I decided that when I was about ten feet above the water, I'd pull the nose up as much as possible to ease the plane onto the surface of the waves. Just before that, I'd open the canopy. The force of the air, as the plane fell, would tear it from the fuselage. I'd have to duck to make sure it didn't hit me. Then I'd release the harness buckles. Then, after the plane sank, I'd be alone in the water until exhaustion overcame me.

I still sensed no desire to live, but I thought perhaps I might be able to steer the plane into a glide that might bring me near to one of the bright blue boats I'd seen before. I hadn't made up my mind to do this, but it was still possible.

In waking life, I could smell the cold salt mist and hear the rushing of the sea. I felt a pervasive but not unmanageable undercurrent of danger and intense sadness. I looked out the window at a clear blue sky bright with diffused golden sunlight. For a while I was still a Japanese man flying a stolen airplane.

8

TWILIGHT AND HISTORY

for Margaret Lucy Federico

1)

Winter night and slippers. Instability on the icy driveway. Well, there's a reason they call them slippers. Slippery bed slippers. She should be slipping into bed. Or, determined as she was, she should have put on the boots. Even with having to sit down and bend and the shortness of breath and the undignified tugging at slippery boot tops in the freezing hallway. Why did coldness make indignity worse? Well, it did. It does. Oh, she'd thought, she'd just run out for a second and get... what was it? He'd called from the hospital. He'd asked for something.

Years and years of joyful marriage and it came to this. Him almost paralyzed in the piss-smelling rehab center. Her, a guest in some distant cousin's house. Him wanting... oh just wanting... more time together... a bit more time, but asking for... what was it... a book, a pen, a t-shirt, a magazine. Something she'd left in the car.

And yes, she'd bring whatever it was, that thing, but really all she had to offer any more was raddled, crazy lasting love.

She'd forgotten and crept down the frozen porch steps, crept across the icy driveway. Very very slippery. Stupid. But it would just take a second. She'd gotten away with worse. Often.

SHITSHITSHIT

It says itself rapidly, she's careening fast as a comet falling earthward through the dark night sky. She's falling, whoopsie-daisy: even now she can see the humor of it as her legs slip from under her. She begins to laugh as the hard bright ice looms up fast.

SHIT and

CONK!!!

Waves of burning yellow-green light sear. Seas of cold blackness break in one giant shot of pain over all the history in her old head. Words all gone. Except for a whispered:

Good Bye, Sweetie.

Oh my love, she thinks.

Darkness.

                            *

Now she's in the depth of the sea, ever rolling, touched and pressed by currents, warmer, cooler, moving. And the sounds, the resonant hollow songs drifting within currents, rising and falling on thermal shifts. Songs of vast migrations hidden in the dark.

*

A little girl saw the great blue whale in the Museum of Natural History. She wore a gray-blue tweed coat with a blue velvet collar. On wires, it was floating in the air.

Now the great blue whale is swimming in the ocean darkness. Water touching every inch of gray-blue skin, conveying warmth and cold and song and in the forebrain the subtler impulses of magnetic poles. Rippling down, down through the sea, echoes of distant stars or pathways of moonlight or laughing expanse of bright and warming sun.

It's all evolving around her: new kinds of living sea.

Sensation and skin inseparable. Inner/outer unmediated. This great singing warmblood is the ocean's mind. Its heart is audible far off as the shimmery krill filters in the baleen with tons of water, the great whale moving easily. Moving unseen deep below the surface. Effortlessly nourished. Vast and silent. Barely moving, deep at ease.

*

Mind.

Moving gently within its own realm. Inseparable in darkness.

The great singer, the great knower, knowing something one does not wish to end, even as one begins to sense perhaps it is a dream. An inner warmth pervasive. A leisurely stretch of fin. A movement that does not feel like movement, continuing in darkness.

But now she moves, and there is pain: pain and cold cold skin. She tries to let go of the particulars, to sift down into the easy depths. Almost.

Time has passed. A lot of time. How does she know? She knows.

Something sparkles.

From here,

Seen across the glassy curve,

From the green arched back of the ingoing wave,

The brittle shore is so unimaginative,

So stolid and sad,

Its denizens so angular and conscious.

*

She is resistant but she knows. She knows if she stays in the darkness, she will remain in darkness.

Living in a world she can share will soon not be an option.

She sighs. Stretches. Shooting stars of pain. Don't open your eyes.

She moves. It hurts.

2)

Moving, she knows. She is trapped in a very old body, rusted, frozen, crusty, musty, dusty, old. Lifting her head slightly, she wants to vomit. She does not want to open her eyes. Knows she must.

Open your eyes, you sleepy head. Time to get up.

Time to get up. She sighs, She can smell her own sour breath lingering on the ice. Bad gums.

Wait. Just for a moment more, don't move. Stay.

She forgot something.

A mermaid in the sea, yes, how could she have forgotten.

*

She who for a glance of the earth-bound life, so yearned that she sloughed off her silvery skin, shimmering muscular body, her iridescent fins, her ability to fly and twist and dart and hover in the moving tides beneath the sea. To leap above the sea. To spin and glide. To hover in the dark water and drift on eddies and currents. To give that up for feet and gawky and bifurcated pale dry legs and pain and pain of walking on those bony feet.

And surrendered her dark red tongue that trilled in flowing water-sounds moving subtly through the sea to be heard where all of skin is a tympanum. Or emitted fluid melismatic streams or laughs that tickled. Tongue gone, she could no more make shapes within the dry sea of air. Mute.

And breathing too. That harsh, thin and abrasive air. The nourishing fluids of the salten sea left behind. No going back.

The bargain she made, terrifying, terrifying as she said yes she would do it. She trembled. She saw the arid void ahead and she was rushing headlong into an error without love, or solace. She remained faithful. She clung to that single glimpse, that single moment of desire that one flash of one kind of love embodied in a man who walked along the shore barefoot, muscular runner's legs, musing, learned and full of savoir faire, oblivious to her presence not ten feet away in the waves.

But she did it, no matter what. A magic spell became an invisible knife. It drove deep onto her. It cut beneath the silver scales, her legs, parting them. It carved feet and toes from waving frond-like fins. She was cut apart and re-shaped. Mute. She could no longer express the screams that writhed within her. Through silent waves of excruciating pain, she walked awkwardly on land.

Now lying on the ground, she's old. She groans. Even if it means entering further in a world of earth and death, she rolls slightly to her side and presses against the ice. Moving, she feels her body pull down, down, down. She sobs. She knew the truth when her mother first read her the story of the mermaid.

3)

FIAT LUX.

She snaps on the light. She's made it. She's back indoors, and it's warm. She's still cold, wet-bottomed, bruised, butt-sore: these are testaments to skootching up the frozen wooden steps. But she's warm. How long was it? How on earth did she do it?

LIGHTS ON!   SAVED!   WHEEE!

Blinded, dizzy, the wall holds her up. Dazzled, she looks across an expanse of gleaming white marble to the array of designer pots and pans displayed on the smooth glass stove-top. Pretentious. Oh, yes, her hostess, very kind, really. No style even so. But the brass and copper rounded tops shine like the domes of Saint Mark's. Saint Mark's horses? Where are they? Off galloping in the dark.

Something inside her eyes rises like fog, a cloud. Beyond this, born on the solid sheen of pots and pans, a faint and magical other-worldly cathedral with gilded domes and shining orbs arises from the mist, rises from the sea. Rose pink marble walls in their variegated splendor, pointed arches, strange like nothing else. Glamour and the slight smell of rotting fish.

A short skinny priest in black and a wide brimmed hat opens the great door. It is a fiery oven inside. The gilded tiles glow like embers A young girl emerges, genuflects, turns to leave. She bumps into the priest. His hand touches her breast. The girl glares. Someone giggles. Somewhere further off, she hears an old woman sigh, a Bridge of Sighs, she sighs.

And behind her, she feels the great open square, a huge public reception room whose ceiling is the sky:

Tiepolo clouds, eternally stylish, crisp and repetitive symmetrical marble facades, gilded cafes. Everyone's invited. When she'd been there, she was so small. Carnival. A dream filled with masked characters. St. Mark's Square. Commedia del Arte. How does it go?

Olivia at her window plays a love scene with Flavio standing in the street below. Flaminia, at her window around the corner argues with Orazio, as their love affair ends. An old man cackles lecherously. Let's go to the theater, she hears her husband laughing. And they did often. Sitting in the dark and snuggled as the actors raved.

Oh, she's getting dizzy again. She's cold and wet. Tea would be just the thing. Yes. Turns on the electricity below the teakettle that now looks exactly like St. Mark's. Beautiful. So tired she is. She stands on the little carpet in front of the stove. Shivers in her wet nightie Exhausted. Sleeps standing up. Dreams of clouds cities, domes, the theater of the world.

4)

Dreams of fluffy-tufty steam clouds billowing up and up in puffy rounded pillows, then ... nothing.

A white, late morning, seaside sky, void. Pleasant. Warm on the front.

The steamship is in the pale green bay about to dock. The voyage is over.

Water lapping at the pier.

Ooooh and a horrible burning chemical smell.

Vile and man-made;

An oil refinery puking on the shore, puking out smoke, a counter-billowing to those white tufty ones. These are stinky streams of smoke polluting the air with some awful inhuman acrid...SHIT ...OH SHIT ... OH NO.

She wakes completely, standing there. The kettle has burned through. The splendid, gold-domed kettle. The ex-Saint Marks. Maybe she forgot to put in the water. She turns off the heat beneath the smooth black glass. And remembers...

Remembers her hostess very proud of this teapot. Made a point of showing it. "It's in the design collection at MOMA" Looks down modestly." Oh it's ok to use it. That's what it's for." Said, brightly, indulgently. Then told her the name of the designer... Italian.. and the cost.... terrible. That's what it's for...

Oh, shit shitshit. Now her hostess will really have to be kind. Unbearably kind. More blessed to give than to receive? Not in this case. Receiving all that benevolent forgiveness? A tiny trip to hell.

Or maybe this will be the final straw. Her charming hostess will reveal some Godzilla creature that's lurked forever deep beneath the seas waiting to be born and then Pow! stomping on cities, evicting self. Ooof. How to know? What is to be done?

Well, amends must be made and pronto. Where's her purse?

For once the world is in a cooperative mood and leaves it for her on the table by the door.

Is it really going to help? She rummages. YES, her wallet is there. And credit cards.

She tiptoes to the family room. No more family, that's why they can put her up now. She turns on the light. The beige leather overstuffed sofa invites her like a fat lady to sit in her lap. Goody.

But she remembers the remote. Proud of herself. Clicks the thing. A blare of sound. Oooops. She turns it down fast. Proud of having even this iota of technological skill. Made it work. Her head aches like crazy, but she can still manage. HAH There it is. Out of the white fluorescent glare. A world is shaping up. Glittering. She's made it. It's going to work.

Yes. Thank God. The Home Shopping Channel. And thank god they're selling housewares, not jewelry or sewing machines or automotive stuff.

A silver-plated tea service, shining cheap and like chrome. Antique federal design, they say, pops up, lingers, numbers whirl, tea service gone, supplanted by, what..... crystal candy dish?

A parade of shiny objects displayed in even bright white light, robbing them of any life if ever they'd had it. But showing them bristling with brittle, available aggressiveness, ready to enter your home. While the voices of a sporty enthusiastic young man and the accommodating and helpfully interested women describe said object in the most flattering ways. How beautiful. How useful. How impressive. Your friends will all... well, yes they have to, don't they?

Who cares? For the moment it's enough just to be here in this bazaar made of crystal white light and metallic sound.

Amends can now be made even before the loss is discovered. A new kettle.

And is the phone still where it was last night on the table at the end of the couch. YES.

The world is still showing it's kindly face. WHEEEEEE. Her ship's come in. And it's like sailors are rolling crates and crates of goodies down the gangplank past her wondering eyes. Her eyes overcome by sleep. The parade of bright objects brought from afar for her delectation. Choices. But sleep also is now choiceless. She's slipped and drifts into the world protected by St. Mark's extravagant dome. Wandering on rain slick black pavement of Venice's streets, she's sure something marvelous may happen amid this salty hint of sadness.

The TV chatters on, there is a flickering outside her eyeballs. The pulse of objects following on and on brings a loneliness, a feeling of standing outside a store-window in the rain and looking in where all is bright and clean and clear... Sadness. And the thread of tinny chatter. Oh, as she begins to slide into kindly misty darkness, but feels the sorrow and loneliness of living amid the panoply of things. Their inhuman definiteness. They are what they are. She looks at them, but they do not look back. There is no mutual regard. Oh, but this tension can be resolved: "Buy me. I'll be yours. No questions asked."

Then, a tender miracle, an older mellow voice has drifted up from the fog. It's familiar, and she's not afraid. Her husband is walking companionably beside her, speaking. He's a dapper dandy and she loves his cologne which is not the cheap kind. His scent like white irises on an overcast afternoon. His voice American southern with a touch of Oxford, mannerly. He's picked up old world culture. His like is not likely to return. He's telling her how, in the 19th century, they ended night. Gas lamps then neon and incandescent bulbs. Soft and warm. They're walking towards the Arsenale. Cold and mist make lights so promising. He is narrating it all.

He's narrating the world out there. A world of things. Things that are waiting, things that can change, things that can change you, your life. They move through the streets. The windows are bright with things.

Beautiful leather goods, glass candelabras, peau de soie, egret plumes, malacca canes, black silk hats, a platinum brooch, a Moire dressing gown....Oooh.

Aha, there it is. On the screen. That's it. Fully awake, huntress ready to strike. She lurches for the phone, knocks it off the end table. She pulls herself together. Carefully grabs her credit card, remote control, slides to the floor. Streeeeetch. She's got the phone just as they say the number to call. Fate has intervened. She manages the transaction. Gives the address. She's done it. She's upheld the proprieties. A replacement for the thing that burned. Her hostess will soon receive... shit!.. well, something, something nice.

Exhausted, she lays head down on arm, pulls up feet, sighs, Oh My, starts to cry. What on earth did she buy? For the life of her she can't remember. She falls asleep. She feels she is sinking through the sparkling surface of a warm dark sea. People are nearby. It's not unpleasant. She is adrift, drifting down on dimming lights, distant voices, suggestive words, on... on and on.

5)

It's dark. The historic theater has a gilded amplitude. She smells layers of familiar perfumes. There's a pleasant buzz of whispered conversation. The play is about to begin. She can feel the audience around her but cannot see them. She's dissolving in a comfortable feeling of shared anticipation. His hand reaches in the dark for hers. Squeezes gently.

With a whoosh, the curtains part. And... the stage is dark. In the dim chiaroscuro, she can barely see the set. It's a dungeon filled with men. Ill and exhausted, they lie, sit, lean against the walls. They wear tattered 18th century military uniforms. At either side of the stage, there is an officer in fresh dress array with epaulettes, gold frogging, shiny boots, fancy tricorn hat. Captain Bravento and Captain Spavento. As one paces, the other tells stories to rouse or impress the wasted troops. Each ignores the other, acts as if the other is invisible and inaudible. They alternate, one pacing as the other declaims, and tell their stories as rapidly as possible.

Bravento:

Rescued by the jailer's daughter, I made my way through mountain passes, was enslaved by a mandarin who later adopted me and sent me via the great Yellow River through hundreds of splendid towns and cities to Xanadu, the dazzling maroon walled capital of China.

Spavento:

I marched through steamy, insect ridden jungles, was attacked by savage indians and wounded twice by their arrows.

Bravento:

There I was honored by the Emperor, Kublai Khan. I became a trusted advisor. I had a tile-roofed palace, silk robes, hundreds of blue and white porcelain bowls, silver spoons, gold trays and lacquer boxes. I had six wives and twenty-six slaves.

*

Her mind slows, filled with luxury and visions of silky clouds, towering palaces, winding gardens, men in brocade robes, dancing girls, jade ewers, pottery horses, dark eyes staring out from cinnabar lattice, lotus blossoms on a lake, jeweled bracelets, paintings of misty mountains, cinnamon. They almost conceal the fetid smell of sewage flowing in the river just beneath.

*

Bravento (interrupts these reveries):

Eventually I yearned for home. I packed up all my treasures, disguised myself as a merchant, hid gems in my robes and silkworms in my rice. But on arriving back in Venice, all my goods were seized to satisfy creditors I had never heard of.

Spavento:

I killed hundreds and hundreds of the savages, invaded their stone cities, saw their altars sticky with the black blood of human sacrifice, received my portion of gold. With gold whose hot reflected luster burns in the eye, with a room full of gold capable of transforming itself into the object of any desire, I returned home to Venice.

*

In the dark, she finds herself thrilled. The audience is thrilled. They can smell the gold-lust, the sweat of impenitent greed. It's a terrifying glee that rises from the blood-hot yellow refulgence of bars of gold, as all scruples are crushed and all barriers conquered. A world of riches. Why hold back?

Bravento:

They swore I'd taken their money. So enraged was I at these liars that I struck one with my sword and killed him. I was puzzled that I was then accused, not of murder but of swindling.

Spavento:

Buying what I wanted, buying friendship and admiration, I lived like a lord. I reveled in the tasseled beds of courtesans. My money ran out. I borrowed and gambled 'til no one knew me anymore. I was enraged when they arrested me for murder. That's one crime I never committed.

*

As they tell their stories with ever more extravagant gestures, the prisoners giggle, groan, sigh. The two captains move slowly towards each other at the center of the stage. A door opens and a shaft of light illuminates their faces. They are identical twins. She gasps. Her husband laughs delighted. The audience sighs in amazement.

*

The two Captains turn and stare directly at her. There's a foul smell. She is looking up at them eye to eye. Her mind is blank, She grasps her husband's hand. He's not there. She'd lost him in all these stories and things. She panics.

She rolls over and wakes suddenly.

Oh no, no, no, she's peed and shit in her nightgown.

*

Help me. Help me.

*

She phones him. She knows he can't help. He's half asleep, He's miles away. He's a wreck and can't much move, doesn't mind, even in the depth of night, being waked up. It's all a dream he sometimes says. A nightmare really. And he laughs. What else is there to do but laugh. He can't help her at all. Not at all, and they both know it.

"The wicked witch," he sings out to her. "The wicked witch has got me now." She loves him no less even now nobly laughing in his prison of himself. Himself and age. Time and flesh plus unstable bones and crinkly nerves.

"Oh yes," he carols, "she's got me and she'll keep me. And ridiculous it may be but she'll work her way with me in this absurdity 'til I'm gone gone gone." He had somehow managed to break his leg and now he's stoned on Demerol. His mind is a carnival of theater from middle ages and on. "I love you," he says uncharacteristically. "The Wicked Witch of the West has got me now. And I love you forever. I'm stuck. I'm doomed. I'm fucked out of luck. But it's you I love and always and no other." She cries because she knows it's true and he almost never says it. "Come, get into bed with me. Come Come. Come." He chants. His voice emerging from the phone like it was rattling down a long sewer pipe. Growing fainter?

"Oh. Oh. Oh." She cries. "I can't come. I can't see you. I can't. My blood pressure's gone crazy. The Doctors say that when I see you, off it goes. Off the charts." This is true even if it makes no sense.

"Oh, my love. The wicked witch has got me and I can't escape."

"Please..." She begins to cry.

"Mercy me. Oh no. Don't cry. Come into my arms.

Do come. It's now.

Will we live together? Let's try. We can manage a little longer. Don't you think?" They both are crying.

He knows, she thinks. He knows. The witch that's caught him in her net and is holding him in a world he'd rather leave, that witch that bitch, that wicked witch of the west, which old witch? The wicked witch: that one holding him here is me.

He'll never admit it, she knows. They can torture him. They are torturing him. He'll never say it.

Well, if he won't, I won't. There's nothing to say. Who can explain it, anyhow?

So amid the cold wet urine, the smell of shit, she rolls over, back to sleep. Yes, her hostess will find her thus on the soiled maybe ruined sofa. Let her deal with it. The filth, the embarrassment, the everything. It's her problem now. Someone else's. She sighs happily.

In sleep, she laughs.

She laughs sliding down a greasy hill, shiny in the sun. It's history, she says to herself. Falling into the all-encompassing chaos of the world, like sliding into a ruined city, or a melted banana split, laughing or sobbing too as the chaos absorbs her. She's history.

9.

SOLDIER CRY

FOR JOAN ANDERSON AND ROBERT SPELLMAN

I

Heaven divides the world:

In dark and light,

In night and day,

In the living and the dead.

Only in the movement of sun, moon and stars

Do we know ourselves.

We know ourselves only

As a moment of light between fleeting clouds.

Beneath the vast bright sky,

The living dwell in their villages and homes.

In fathomless shadow,

The dead inhabit their silent towns.

Now the living surround the Eastern capital.

Now the dead surround the Western hills.

Though inseparable,

The living and the dead

No longer know each other.

In moments of joy,

They do not remember the other,

In bitterness,

They do not long for one another.

(1)

II

The cold passes reluctantly from the earth, and the
retreating mists reveal an army stretched out for miles
on the hills, asleep. A watery sun rises slowly and the
landscape changes from pale gray to green. The army
stirs. It trembles at the whispers of rumor. It casts its
eyes upon the roads.

(2)

III

With a groan, I start from sleep.

All the earth is on the march to war.

The rulers have commanded it.

*   (3)

Heaven is high and far away.

The king's business never ends.

I cannot stay to plant my crops

How will my parents and my children live?

Heaven is high and far away.

The earth below must always march to war.

When will it end?

We pray for a sovereign.

We pray the sacrifices he commands

Bring peace.

Yet we long for home.

In what month will we return?

(5)

No breeze stirs.

We must wait.

I look down the highway

And my heart is blank.

(6)

*

Oh bright Heaven high above,

Shining on the earth below,

How our westward march

Has brought us to the empty plains.

We have suffered cold and heat.

Oh the aching of an empty heart.

Oh the poisons of bitterness.

Thinking of the ones who raised us,

My tears fall like rain in the sadness of my heart.

Though I long for life and home,

I cannot turn back.

Warfare drags me on.   (7)

IV

The sweat of waiting, even in the silent cold; even
those who can't stop talking, each is frozen in his own
thoughts, frozen, choking in the rank smell of fear
and dust.

Now slowly, like a moving flood-gate,

Iron scraping iron,

The great hinge of battle opens.

At the shout of command, there is no longer any
time. Doubts dissolve in the sheer mass charge: arms
taut, weapons held in front, legs pumping, screaming

war cries.

Wildly, we shout:

Seu Lhawang Damsang, ride with me.

Tungsen Karma, keep me strong.

Nyengen Deva, be my shield.

Shinje Chogyal, do not fail me.

Seu Thuchen Mongpa, guide my arm.

Enemies rise up like weeds before us. They are cut down. Again they rise. Again we cut them down. The long day's work of killing has begun.

Charging, shouting, scrambling wildly down the hillside, slashing right and left amid the hail of arrows and bullets, then, the clear bitter smell of crushed leaves and blood, the exhilaration of running, and cold air pouring through nostrils. Everything is desperately alive, and it is impossible to imagine this torrent of life can ever end.

V

A bow string snaps,
Suddenly nothing moves.
The world swirls around us in a dazzling whirlwind.
At its center, time stops.

The white disc of a single cloud
Hovers in the pale sky.

Flocks of sparrows rise and wheel.
Red, yellow and black banners flutter.

Sunlight glitters

On steel blades and spear points.

Sword arms raised, mouths gaping,

Soldiers freeze.

An arrow stops in mid-flight.

VI

Now shining like diamonds in the air,

The gods of war hear our cry.

They descend in a circle of hard light,

Seated on their steeds of wind,

Indifferent to all obstacles and enemies.

Radiant

They do not waver.

While everything around them now erupts

In wave on wave of sundered flesh and horror:

Soldiers forget their names, their home.

They charge on as if there were no death.

They do not think.

They throw themselves onto the red teeth of war.

And now

The living and the dead

Part.

The world of the living bursts open.

The world of the dead falls into the black earth.

VII

Now amongst the living

There is, for a moment, exhilaration.

There is lawless abandon.

Now, there is, for a moment, feasting, drinking, delirium.

No limit can be placed on the desire to live.

The war gods, sated, return to their abodes.

Then behind us there is silence
Behind us, there are the dead.

They rest in the soft earth on the hills
They, in tens of thousands,
The victors and the vanquished.

They have entered the dark world.
They are cut off from the living,
Their tomb is sealed.

In their joy, they do not remember one another,
In their bitterness they do not long for one another.

(8)

*

Beneath a hard and barren sun,

I climb the ridge of a high mountain

Alone to wander home.

In passing, I look down on the capital.

Its walls are shattered,

Its palaces and houses burnt to ash.

Its royal names effaced from looted tombs,

Family homes and gravestones now in ruins

No hearth fires, no offerings

A thousand miles without chimney smoke.

There is no one,

No trees, no grass,

No birds, nor birdsong.

There is silence.

I have been away too long.

I cannot find a pathway back

Where I, my parents, wife, my children

Lived our lives.

There are no shadows.

Memories have faded.

There is no path before me.

Gone.

I turn inward.

Alive or dead,

I can no longer say.   (9)

VIII

In the torrent of existing,

In the fires of endless war,

We have touched

The all-consuming heart.

The blazing sky embraces the dark earth.

Our eyes are scorched.

We are immobile.

Words have no meaning.

Parted,

The living and the dead

Hold the secret of fleeting love.

They do not know peace.

10. THE COMING OF THE ICE AGE :

DREAMS AND SINGS THE MINOTAUR

IN HIS MAN-MADE ABODE

for Kidder Smith

I

I.1

Cold is seeping deep into the earth. Freezing drafts
descend, whistling through pipes and vents. In his cellar-
prison, there are no longer corners free from chill. His
feeling of abandonment swells. The cold is fracturing his
mind, his memory. Meaning, like a huge sheet of ice on a
lake, is cracking, breaking of its own frozen intensity.
Deep in the dark and his madness, the Minotaur sings:

Chef barbarismus diety spielt

Dum ter tremendum oni swat

Triumphante imperio divo

On fat roller rubis puis aeternitas

Trashans ter triumphante iti

Mors Habet voluntate final

Entirety ever - me, me, me!

Non postulans mihi hearing end no more

Puisance entiretate mihi

In aeternam eater silence vast sublime.

I.2

His arias and recitatives echoing in the ever tighter
labyrinth of his imprisonment are the last resistance to
frozen abandonment. The mocking light of the pale sun
and the chill blue of the full moon fall directly into his
prison through deep shafts. He prefers shadow and its
memories. The muffled voices of men and women and
children crying, laughing, lying, trickle down through the
vents. They are afraid. Their words return to him in
dreams. He tells himself stories and he sings.

In the darkness of the night, he performs all the parts,
sings all the roles. He repeats his little operas over and
over. His bellowing and anguish, so strangled and deep

prevent men, women, children from coming near the
shafts where he can be heard. Throughout the city his
echoes produce unease. The world will turn to ice. These
are the songs still throbbing at its core.

I.3

The Minotaur knows songs and stories. Who he learned
them from, he cannot recall. He recalls a man's voice
telling him a history. To remind himself that there is time,
that still there may be time, the Minotaur whispers;

Thousands of years ago, King Ashoka conquered the
earth. The memory of betrayals and the absence of love
had blackened his heart. Rage fueled his conquest. When
all nations lay at his feet, he decided to build a replica of
the world he possessed.

He summoned the greatest architects, artists and artisans,
stonemasons, joiners, plasterers and painters. He
conscripted tens of thousands of laborers. Thus he erected
a palace unimaginably lavish and irresistibly beautiful. Its

proportions were perfect and harmonious. It had walls of white marble, cinnabar columns, porticoes of multicolored agate, silver doors adorned with emeralds, rubies, sapphires, windows of quartz, and a roof of gold tiles, adorned with spires of alabaster, domes of turquoise, bronze water spouts in the form of dragons, lions, tigers, phoenixes. It had the beauty of the sea at sunset and the mountains at dawn.

But inside the palace, all was shadow, smoke and darkness. It was a labyrinth from which none could escape. Corridors led nowhere, courts were open sewers, nooks were alive with vermin. All who entered found that this palace so outwardly beautiful was actually a vast torture house. The air smelled of blood and excrement. Sobs and muffled screams filled the air. Seeking a way out, they found themselves circling in a maze. They entered huge chambers filled with racks on which people were being pulled apart. Small men used spikes, knives, hammers, saws and every device for inflicting pain on screaming victims tied to posts. Branding irons and red-hot pokers pulled fresh from braziers left no inch of skin unscored. Naked men and women were hurled into cauldrons of boiling water and half-drowned in tanks of freezing water.

From the ceiling, bodies still alive hung from chains on razor hooks and nooses. Everywhere bare-chested sweating men in black hoods wielded strange-shaped metal instruments to tear and break the bodies of women, children, old men and young. It was impossible to shut out the smell and the din. The visitors ran from room to room until they too were caught, tortured, killed.

This was King Ashoka's vision of the world where, entranced by beauty, there was no escape from excruciation, madness and death. He ordered that none who entered here could ever leave. He went to inspect his handiwork, stepped through the gates, and the guards, despite his raging, did not let him leave.

II

The Minotaur strides past the half-frozen vapor in the stone-walled sewers that link the chambers where he rests. He chants in whispered passage, chants to keep some warmth. His singing is grotesque. It is not like the voice of the woman who, he thinks, sang these songs beside a well. Far below, he heard her voice and imagines her elegant

face. He sings so he can imagine, once again, the song
called Dying Fire.

Lost in darkening arcs, suspended sky:

Solar momentary gold-reddening light;

Do we leave anything behind?

Who can change pain and puzzle, life and time?

Fire and love may rise above the empty lake,

A mud flat now, bleak absent reflected light

Stretching like an evening without rain

And drying to a pained expanse

Of hard, heart-broken night.

III

He remembers. He shudders, The Minotaur tries to
explain to himself his suffering. He thinks:

Supreme terror and complete annihilation. All resolutions
and intentions gone. The antipodes of torment now

without meaning. Phenomena appear and disappear. There is no reference point. Nothing binds, no thread, no net. Freezing. There is pain. A rainbow sky of searing intensities without meaning.

The world of the spoken word: memory requires effort, temporary fascination, recalling the useful. Tied in the body's survival. Holding the glory of living. The beauties we have seen, the fear, the splendor, the frozen end.

And so, there are his songs. He tries to sing in the manner of the songs he heard. tries to remember, but each times he sings, he does not know if they are changing. Even in his prison, there is no stability. He howls out a sonnet called Fire of Torment:

Experience burns in the neon signs'
Fevered pulses: red, blue and glass-encased,
Indifferent promptings; tortures that refine
A rage of unreality and race

Across the black junk heap of disused arts

(Images cut out from Passionate Fame)

Blowing on the streets, where excised of hearts

Crazy-blank angry Heads eyeball a game

Of reality reduced to the edge

Of a stimulated pain; a steel blade

Cuts while coming a nipple in a wedge,

Jamming bliss and suffering to evade

The mocking chrome-lit crying cars

Drugged and remembered in a night of stars.

IV

Shivering, he tries to sleep but the world of dreams is even
intolerable, a mirror of the world of those who, dying,
dwell above him. Their world is contracting. As cold
expands, there is less room for life. They plan, they even
joke, but he hears the undertone of terror in their voices.
He leaps up. He stands at the bottom of a shaft, looking

128

upward to the cold stars. He thrusts back his giant heavy head. This is his dream. He roars and whispers. He wants to crack the descending dome of cold. He wants to wake the night. He dreams

IV.1

The little girl is walking down the corridor. It is solid and quiet like the hallways in her school, and she pauses at a half-open door. In the dim oblique light, she sees a cement-walled room. A woman, middle-aged, is strapped to a heavy wooden chair. She is wearing a stained night-gown. The chair is bolted to the floor; the straps are leather, worn. Two sweating men are working on her. They have their backs to the door.

One man lifts a glass gallon bottle of bright red fluid over the woman's head. A black rubber hose is attached to the bottle mouth. The other man, with one hand holds the rubber hose and forces it down the woman's throat. With his other hand, he holds her nose. The red fluid is forced down her throat and into her stomach. She struggles weakly.

IV.2

The little girl watches from the doorway, but the scene
seems very distant. She watches the red water empty from
the bottle into the woman in the chair. The little girl can
imagine the pain; she can feel the woman's stomach
expanding as she swallows rather than drown. Despite the
panic, the woman is too exhausted to do more than wiggle
a little and moan. Urine spatters on the floor. She has
given up hope. There is no answer, no response she can
give that will make the torturers give back her power over
herself. She is at the mercy of others. This will not change..
She is at the mercy of those who have no mercy.

IV.3

The little girl stands in the doorway. She clearly imagines
the pain, the feeling of utter abandonment., but it is far
away. At the far end of the room, she sees a man in a crisp
dark suit sitting at a desk quietly taking notes.

IV.4

The man in the suit looks up. His gaze is curious without
emotion. Standing in the doorway, the little girl feels very
young. Though what she is watching does not now touch
her, she knows, knows absolutely that this can, this will
happen to her one day. The man writing it all down has
seen her.

V

V.1

Frozen, he curls in a corner, rests his bovine furry horned
head on his cold naked knees. Is there finally, some way
to imagine his life of day and night imprisonment, his
endless suffering, his endless loneliness, as having any end
or meaning? His breath is slowing. He is shivering but his
blood is becoming thick with tiny crystals of ice. The
treasure of all his sorrows is a story he heard an old man
tell a boy many years ago. They were standing by the shaft
as the old man recited the tale of the conjured city. Clearly,
the man had memorized it, and it was a very old story.

He listened and, though he did not believe the story, he likewise memorized it. It is now his only solace.

V.2

The great disciple explained: "My master, the Buddha, knew that those who wished to escape from tormented confusion in this life would have to traverse a steep and treacherous path. On their journey, again and again, they would encounter their own attachments and false beliefs. Constantly they would justify their cowardice and delusion. Seeing there how ingrained was their self-deception, they would become disheartened. They would no longer believe they could free themselves or realize the awakened nature. They could not help but wish to stop on their journey. They would say:

'We cannot go further. There is still such a great distance ahead. We want to turn back.'

"Then the Buddha, a man of many stratagems said: 'Don't be afraid! Soon we will reach a great city where you can stop and rest. Later, when you have the strength, you can continue your journey.' Thus encouraged, they continued.

"Soon a city, with high crimson walls and bronze gates came into view. The exhausted travelers were overjoyed. They pressed forward and entered the city. The residents were spiritual people and welcomed the travelers as kinsmen. Broad airy boulevards led to bountiful markets, quiet gardens, libraries, temples, food stalls. Warm breezes carried the scent of spices, faint perfumes, the faint sounds of chanting. The voyagers rested, studied and meditated in comfort. They cultivated spiritual awakening.

"When the Awakened One saw that his students had regained their strength and confidence, he dissolved this splendid city into thin air. Nothing remained but a cold cloudless blue sky, harsh mountains and a faint rocky pathway. The followers looked around in shock. 'The city was a phantom conjured from your desires. The awakened state is as close as your eyelash to your eye.'"

V.3

Roaring, roaring, he cannot stop. He is waiting. He has
heard the stories, the consolations, the words. The
Minotaur knows the hero with his relentless guile and his
frozen steel sword has already entered his heart him.
Death is the sole deliverance fate will grant him. The
Minotaur is immobilized in a story that gave him life. Ice is
covering the world. His world is frozen in a single set of
possibilities. All else are dreams and songs. The Minotaur
is afraid, tormented by the moon, by wishes, by roaring
and unending madness, by ice, by stories he cannot
understand and songs no one else can hear.

11.
CONSCIENTIOUSNESS

In memory of Delbert Riddle

I

"The waiter plays with his condition
in order to attain it." -J.P.Sartre

Without Place or Name
The Body is an object on loan.

Location then
Emergent in the forms of its movement:

Green ocean combed with flecks of white foam,
A sparkling line left on the shore
Where pinpoint holes from buried clams
Pop in the sand on waves' retreat.

Seen then from the boardwalk

As the parched scent rises

Shimmering off the salt-baked planks

Isolated.

And the cool insouciant wave-borne

Breeze tousles a lock of hair

Here.

A sparkle of air

That requires elegance,

White slacks, white shoes,

A straw hat

For its fulfillment.

So that you would appear.

You

Imagined further.

II

"Mind is absorbed into the desired object as oil is absorbed into cloth." - *Geshe Gyatso on Shantideva*

Expanded

The skin of the bathers,

Shrimp pink and tender,

Encounters on its tightened surfaces

The cold sea.

Hairs in their puckered follicles

Stand on end.

The message of contraction,

Received with oooo and ssss.

The teased bathers leap

Surrender

Take the plunge.

The float, sated and sustained

In rise and gentle fall

Aaaaah. Say,

Is this returned

Or yearning?

From here,

Seen across the glassy curve,

The green arched back of the ingoing wave,

The brittle shore is so unimaginative,

So stolid and sad,

Its denizens so angular and conscious.

As for a time

Of wave-borne ease

The bathers yet

Do not renounce a common fate.

Given

Love then innate in circumstance.

You.

III

*"In the unhappy realms of sickness, bondage and
the shedding of blood..." - Shantideva*

Gifts given

Are so difficult to receive

Wrapped in implication,

Portents, messages.

From a distant radio

The splendid open voice

Of the great tenor

Long dead, glides on

Gilding the evening's air

Encore.

Inscribing pleasure's promise

On the inner ear

And vanishment.

A flickering compromise

With what cannot be appeased

By the solo pure exhale.

IV

"As though hypnotized by a spell, I shall reduce this mind

to nothing. Even I do not know what is causing me

confusion. What is there dwelling inside me?" - Shantideva

Reliant

On the green and cool emergent,

The pliant,

The delightful

Givens in immediacy

Which seen

In the angled light of sunset

Crystallize

As a martyrology

Of those who must labor, walk and eat

In the sorrow of necessity,

Burned by the secret of absolution

Pouring from the heart

Of a reddening copper sun.

A pure yearning

Requiring the body to be destroyed

In the untouchable donation

Of a wounded mind

Whose love, though unabsolved

Attains a piercing moment

Of luminous splendor

In returning to silence.

V

"Then if my body blazes for a long time..." – *Shantideva*

But the Grasping Masters,

Rulers over earth and sea,

Eye, ear, tongue and touch

Contrive to unify

In legal speech

A Roman Emperor's feast:

A menu of minute discernments,

Base omnivorous intrigues

From an addicted lust,

Not to quality event or sense,

But to location sole,

Ultimate, continuous, complete.

And the globe so articulated

Under momentary single rule

Is glamorized in the lurid assertion

Of meaning fated realized.

Of this,

Even

The ruin, the bleached wall

Stands with muted gleam

On the headland of the shore;

Does not witness rise and fall,

Remains a partial lustrous monument;

Remains

The implicate fragment.

O unappeased of incomplete continuing.

NOTES

2) CONTINUING WITH: ARAKAWA

EMBODIED EFFIGIES- - winter 1/12

http://effigiesmag.com/archives/issue-two/

(1) citation from Arakawa: 'Some Words,pp37-39 Stadtische Kunsthalle Dusseldorf, 1977

3) ELEMENTS

THE LOST COUNTRY – Winter 2014/2015

http://www.inexsilio.com

4) DREAM TIGER (BY THE RIVER) -

ANNAK SASTRA - 2/20/12

http://anaksastraarchive.wordpress.com/issue-7-april-2012/

5) TIME'S UNENDING was commissioned by Diane Betkowski and the Denver Eclectic Concerts and first performed 1/12/12 preceding Olivier Messiaen's Quatuor Pour La Fin du Temps

Published in ATTICUS REVIEW , May1, 2014

http://atticusreview.org/times-unending/

6) ELYSIUM -

DANSE MACABRE 65- 12/18/12-1/7/13

http://dansemacabreonline.wix.com/dm-archiv#!__dm-65/fictions/vstc13=elysium

7) YOU DIED, AND -

MARCO POLO ARTS MAGAZINE 1/12/12

http://www.marcopoloartsmag.com/You-Died-And

8) **TWILIGHT HISTORY** -

CONTRARY - Fall 2012/Winter 2013

http://contrarymagazine.com/2012/twilight-histories-a-monologue/

Adapted for performance with Deborah Marshall at The Taos Salon- with thanks to Abbie Conant and William Osborne

9) **SOLDIER CRY**

Performed as an installation piece for Joan Anderson at Naropa Institute and later with Deboarah Marshall at the Taos Studio

Adaptations from: (1) Mark Edward Lewis- The Creation of Space in Early China; SUNY 2007- p.123 (2) Stephen Crane- The Red Badge of Courage Chapter1, p.1)3)Arthur Waley tr. The Book of Songs:Grove Press:1301;4)#152;(5)#151;(6)#150;(7)#149(8)#139;(9)#133; 10)#148;(11)#146;(12)#143;(13)#141;(14)#130-1(15) Lewis- supra, p. 123(16) Cao Zhi, son of Cao Cao- Lewis, supra.-p.188

10) **THE COMING OF THE ICE AGE**

THE GONE LAWN JOURNAL #16 OCTOBER17, 2014

http://journal.gonelawn.net/issue16/Penick.php

11) **CONSCIENTIOUSNESS**

FAT CITY REVIEW- 8/30/13

http://fatcityreview.com/conscientiousness-douglas-penick

*

Author photograph by Martin Fritter

Douglas Penick was a research associate at the Museum of Modern Art, NY, and studied and practiced with Chogyam Trungpa, Rinpoche and other Tibetan teachers for more than 40 years. He wrote the Canadian NFB's series on the Tibetan Book of the Dead (Leonard Cohen, narrator) and libretti for two operas: King Gesar (Sony CD w/ Ma, Serkin, Ax, etc.) and Ashoka's Dream (Santa Fe Opera) with Peter Lieberson. He received grants from the Witter Bynner Foundation for Poetry and from the Graham Foundation. In addition to three book-length episodes from the Gesar Epic, many of his short pieces have been published in the US, Canada, Malaysia, the UK, France, the Czech Republic, Hungary, India, Germany and Australia. His novel about the 3rd Ming Emperor, JOURNEY OF THE NORTH STAR, was brought out by Publerati in 2012 DREAMERS AND THEIR SHADOWS, his new novel about spiritual seekers, teachers and the labyrinth of their longings, became available in 2013. He is married to the renowned clarinetist, Deborah Marshall.